D0754716

JOHNNY DEPP

Maggie Murphy

PowerKiDS press.

New York

Published in 2011 by The Rosen Publishing Group, Inc.
29 East 21st Street, New York, NY 10010

First Edition

Editor: Jennifer Way
Book Design: Kate Laczynski

Photo Credits: Cover Jason Merritt/FilmMagic/Getty Images; pp. 4, 6, 27 (top) Shutterstock.com; p. 5 Vince Bucci/Getty Images; p. 7 Chris Gordon/Getty Images; p. 8 Frank Micelotta/Getty Images; p. 9 Barry King/WireImage/Getty Images; p. 10 Hulton Archive/Getty Images; p. 11 Fotos International/Getty Images; p. 12 Jim Smeal/ WireImage/Getty Images; p. 13 Darlene Hammond/Getty Images; pp. 14–15 © 20th Century Fox Film Corp./courtesy of Everett Collection; p. 16 Ron Galella, Ltd./WireImage/ Getty Images; p. 17 Junko Kimura/Getty Images; pp. 18, 20 Getty Images/Handout/ Getty Images; p. 19 Dave Hogan/Getty Images; p. 21 David Appleby/AFP/Getty Images; p. 22 Pascal Le Segretain/Getty Images; pp. 23, 26, 27 (bottom), 28 Kevin Winter/Getty Images; pp. 24–25 © Walt Disney/courtesy of Everett Collection; p. 29 Frazer Harrison/ Getty Images; p. 30 Andrea Pattaro/AFP/Getty Images.

Library of Congress Cataloging-in-Publication Data

Murphy, Maggie.
Johnny Depp / by Maggie Murphy. — 1st ed.
    p. cm. — (Movie superstars)
Includes webliography and index.
ISBN 978-1-4488-2566-0 (library binding) — ISBN 978-1-4488-2721-3 (pbk.) —
ISBN 978-1-4488-2722-0 (6-pack)
1. Depp, Johnny—Juvenile literature. 2. Motion picture actors and actresses—United States—Biography—Juvenile literature. I. Title.
PN2287.D39M87 2011
791.4302'8092—dc22
[B]
                                    2010033668
Manufactured in the United States of America

CPSIA Compliance Information: Batch #WW11PK: For Further Information contact Rosen Publishing, New York, New York at 1-800-237-9932

Contents

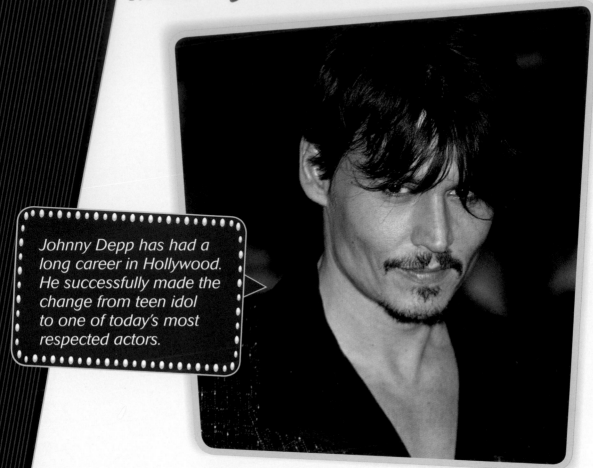

Johnny Depp has had a long career in Hollywood. He successfully made the change from teen idol to one of today's most respected actors.

Johnny Depp is a famous American actor. He has starred in a wide range of movies during his **career**, including *Chocolat* and *Finding Neverland*. Depp is best known for his creative **performances**, such as playing Captain Jack Sparrow in the *Pirates of the Caribbean* movies. He is also famous for his strange

roles in fantasy movies directed by Tim Burton, including *Edward Scissorhands*, *Charlie and the Chocolate Factory*, and *Alice in Wonderland*.

Johnny Depp is considered one of Hollywood's most talented actors. He has been **nominated** for many awards for his acting roles during his career.

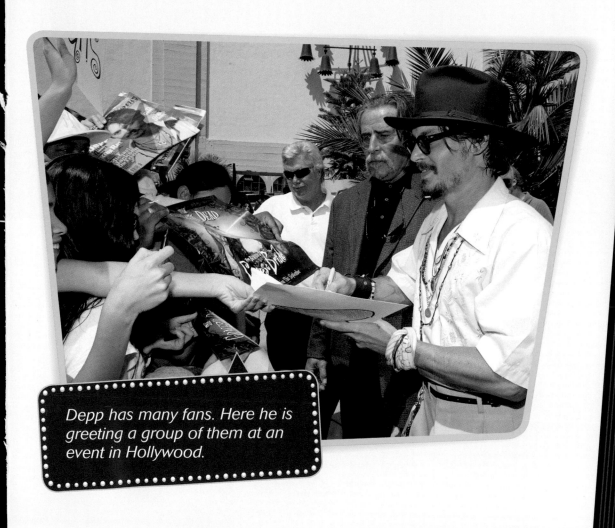

Depp has many fans. Here he is greeting a group of them at an event in Hollywood.

GROWING UP

Johnny Depp moved to Los Angeles, shown here, when he was 20. At the time, his dream was to be a rock star, not an actor.

Johnny Depp was born on June 9, 1963, in Owensboro, Kentucky. His father, John, was a **civil engineer**. His mom, Betty Sue, was a waitress who took care of Johnny and his three older siblings. In 1969, his family moved to

Miramar, Florida. Soon after, his mother bought him a guitar. He quickly learned to play it.

When Johnny was 13, he joined a rock band as a guitarist. Johnny's parents divorced when he was 16. A year later, he left high school to work on his musical career. In 1980, he joined a band called the Kids as their

Depp sings and plays guitar. Here he is in 2007 playing with his old band the Kids.

Here is Depp with his mother, Betty Sue Palmer, at the 2004 Academy Awards.

lead guitar player. The Kids had many fans in Florida and often played for large **audiences**. When Depp was 20, he married his girlfriend, Lori Anne Allison. Soon, he moved to Los Angeles with his band in hopes of becoming famous. Depp wanted to become a rock star.

EARLY ACTING CAREER

Depp's friend Nicolas Cage (left) encouraged Depp to try acting. Here are Depp and Cage in Los Angeles in 1988.

Johnny Depp's band struggled in Los Angeles. After they had been in Los Angeles for a while, Depp's wife met a young actor named Nicolas Cage. She introduced Cage to Depp. Cage convinced Depp to try acting in movies.

Depp's first major film role was in a 1984 horror movie called *A Nightmare on Elm Street*.

In 1986, Depp and his wife divorced. That same year he appeared in a movie about the Vietnam War called *Platoon*. Although Depp's first film roles did not bring him a lot of attention as an actor, he would soon find success in a large role on television.

Johnny Depp's first film role was in A Nightmare on Elm Street. *The movie is about Freddy Krueger, shown here, who kills people by getting into their dreams.*

TEEN IDOL

Depp won many teenage fans while playing Officer Hanson on 21 Jump Street. Depp was on the show from 1987 until 1990.

In 1987, Johnny Depp landed a starring role on a television show, called *21 Jump Street*. The show was a crime drama about young police officers who **specialized** in solving youth crimes. Depp played a police

Here is the cast of 21 Jump Street. *From left to right they are Peter DeLuise, Steven Williams, Dustin Nguyen, Depp, and Holly Robinson.*

officer named Tom Hanson. In the show, the police officers of the 21 Jump Street squad were chosen because they looked very young. This meant they could go undercover to solve crimes by posing as high-school or college students.

21 Jump Street was popular with teenage audiences. It ran on television for five seasons. Depp became *21 Jump Street*'s biggest star. The show brought him a lot of fame and thousands of teenage fans. However, Depp was uncomfortable with the attention of being a teen **idol**. He left the show in 1990, at the end of the fourth season, because he wanted to take more serious acting roles.

Depp and Winona Ryder (right) costarred in the movie Edward Scissorhands. *Here they are in 1990.*

BECOMING A MOVIE STAR

In the early 1990s, Johnny Depp started to choose movie roles that showed off his acting talent. First, Depp starred in a movie called *Cry-Baby* in 1990. *Cry-Baby* is a musical movie set in the 1950s, directed by John Waters. Depp also played the lead role in a movie directed by Tim Burton called *Edward Scissorhands,* in 1990. *Edward Scissorhands*

Depp's character in Edward Scissorhands *is often misunderstood by the people he meets.*

involved **elements** of fantasy, such as Depp's character having scissors for hands. This role brought Depp a lot of attention and respect from movie directors, **critics**, and audiences.

In 1993, Depp starred in a movie called *Benny & Joon*. That same year he also starred in *What's Eating Gilbert Grape* with Leonardo DiCaprio and Juliette Lewis. In this movie, Depp plays a young man who helps take care of his younger brother, who has a mental **disability**. By the mid-1990s, Depp was considered one of Hollywood's rising stars.

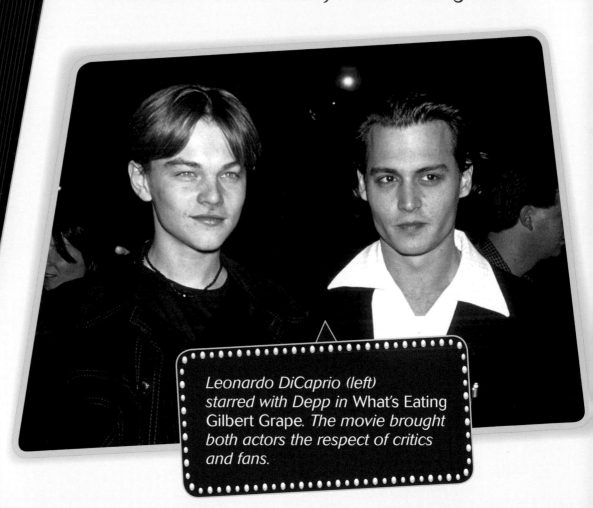

Leonardo DiCaprio (left) starred with Depp in What's Eating Gilbert Grape. *The movie brought both actors the respect of critics and fans.*

TIM BURTON'S MOVIES

Here is Tim Burton (right) with Depp at the Japanese premiere of *Sweeney Todd*.

In 1994, Johnny Depp starred in *Ed Wood*, his second movie with director Tim Burton. Burton had a lot of respect for Depp's creativity as an actor when they worked together on *Edward Scissorhands*. After making *Ed Wood*, Depp and Burton continued to **collaborate** on movies. Their movies are known for being colorful, creative, and often scary.

In Sleepy Hollow, *Depp played Ichabod Crane. Crane is investigating a series of mysterious deaths. Christina Ricci (right) played Katrina Van Tassel, Depp's love interest in the movie.*

In 1999, Depp starred in Burton's *Sleepy Hollow*, based on a story by Washington Irving. He also played the **eccentric** Willy Wonka in 2005's *Charlie and the Chocolate Factory*. Depp also had a voice role in 2005's *The Corpse Bride*, an animated movie made by Burton. In 2007, Depp played the lead role in the musical movie *Sweeney Todd: The Demon Barber of Fleet Street*. Depp collaborated with Tim Burton again when he played the Mad Hatter in 2010's *Alice in Wonderland*. Depp feels that Burton has helped him grow as an artist throughout his career.

Here are Burton and Depp with the cast of Charlie and the Chocolate Factory.

Depp starred in Don Juan DeMarco with Marlon Brando (left), who played his doctor.

During the mid-1990s and early 2000s, Johnny Depp starred in a wide range of movies. These movies included *Don Juan DeMarco*, a romantic comedy in which Depp plays a man who believes he is the legendary Don Juan. In 1997, Depp starred in a crime drama called *Donnie Brasco*. He also appeared in a movie based on a novel by Hunter S. Thompson, called *Fear and Loathing in Las Vegas*, in 1998.

In 1999, Depp played the lead role in a **thriller** called *The Ninth Gate*. He also starred in a **science-fiction** thriller called *The Astronaut's Wife* in 1999. In 2000, Depp appeared in *Chocolat*, a romantic movie.

In Chocolat, *Depp played the love interest of Juliette Binoche's character, a woman who owns a chocolate shop.*

Depp starred in Finding Neverland *with Kate Winslet (right). Here they are with that film's director, Mark Forster (center).*

In 2004, Depp played the role of J. M. Barrie, the creator of the character Peter Pan, in *Finding Neverland*. Kate Winslet also starred in this movie. Like many of his other performances during this time, Depp's performance in *Finding Neverland* brought him a lot of critical attention and award nominations.

PLAYING JACK SPARROW

Although Johnny Depp has played many different movie roles during his career, one of his most famous roles has been the eccentric Captain Jack Sparrow in the *Pirates of the Caribbean* movies. Depp was very involved in deciding how his character would look and act in the movies. Although the *Pirates of the Caribbean* movies are filled with action and adventure, Jack Sparrow is a comedic character

Orlando Bloom, Depp, and Keira Knightley star in the Pirates of the Caribbean *movies.*

SUPERSTAR FACT ⭐

Johnny Depp has 13 tattoos. Each of them stands for something important in his life.

Here is Depp in *Pirates of the Caribbean: Dead Man's Chest, the second movie in the series.*

who is often getting into trouble. Depp has said that he based the character of Jack Sparrow on Keith Richards, the guitarist for the band the Rolling Stones.

The *Pirates of the Caribbean* movies have been huge **box-office** hits and have made Depp even more famous. The idea for the movies came from a Disney theme-park ride. The first movie in the series, *Pirates of the Caribbean: Curse of the Black Pearl,* opened in theaters in 2003. Orlando Bloom and Keira Knightley also had starring

Depp based his Jack Sparrow character on Keith Richards (left). Here are Richards and Depp at an awards show in 2009.

roles in the movie. In 2006, the second movie in the series opened. It was called *Pirates of the Caribbean: Dead Man's Chest*. The third movie, *Pirates of the Caribbean: At World's End*, opened in 2007. In the fourth *Pirates of the Caribbean* movie, Depp costars with Penelope Cruz.

DEPP'S AWARDS

Johnny Depp is one of Hollywood's most respected actors. He has been nominated for many acting awards during his career. He has also won several awards.

Depp has received three Academy Award nominations for Best Actor during his career. He was nominated in 2004 for

Top: *Depp helps promote his movies at film festivals. Here he is at the Venice Film Festival in 2007.* Left: *Depp won the Favorite Movie Actor award at the 2010 People's Choice Awards.*

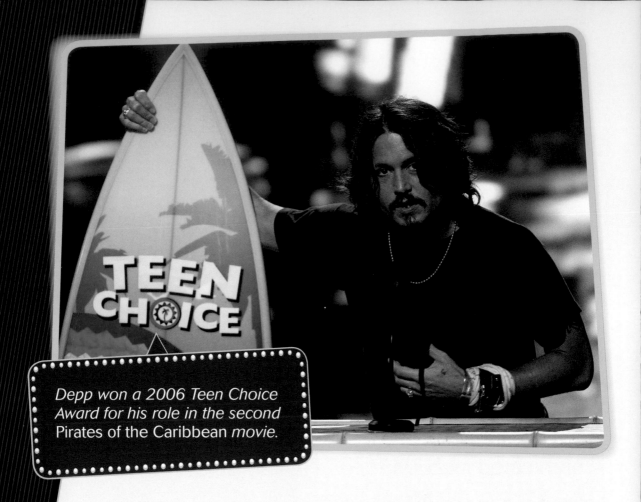

Depp won a 2006 Teen Choice Award for his role in the second Pirates of the Caribbean *movie.*

the first *Pirates of the Caribbean* movie, in 2005 for *Finding Neverland*, and in 2008 for *Sweeney Todd*. He has also been nominated for eight Golden Globe Awards since 1991. He won a Golden Globe in 2008 for his performance in *Sweeney Todd*. Depp has won eight People's Choice Awards, four MTV Movie Awards, and six Teen Choice Awards, too.

FAMILY AND FUTURE

Although Johnny Depp's acting career is very important to him, his family is even more important. Depp has two children with his partner, Vanessa Paradis, a French actress and singer. Their daughter is named Lily-Rose and their son is named Jack. Although Depp often travels to work, he and his family usually live in France.

Depp has been with his partner, Vanessa Paradis, since 1998.

Here is Depp on the set of The Tourist *in Venice, Italy.*

Depp spent the summer of 2010 in Venice, Italy, filming a movie called *The Tourist* with Angelina Jolie. Depp's fans look forward to seeing him star in movies for a long time to come.

⭐ Glossary

audiences (AH-dee-ints-ez) Groups of people who watch or listen to something.

box-office (BOKS-o-fus) Having to do with the money a movie makes.

career (kuh-REER) A job.

civil engineer (SIH-vul en-juh-NIR) Someone who makes plans for public works, such as roads.

collaborate (kuh-LA-buh-rayt) To work jointly toward a common goal.

critics (KRIH-tiks) People who write their opinions about things.

disability (dis-uh-BIH-luh-tee) A condition, such as blindness, that makes someone unable to do certain things.

eccentric (ik-SEN-trik) Strange, different from established ways or styles.

elements (EH-luh-ments) Parts of a whole.

idol (EYE-dul) A person who is greatly loved by his or her fans.

nominated (NOH-muh-nayt-ed) Suggested that someone or something should be given an award or a position.

performances (per-FAWR-ments-ez) The playing of roles in movies, plays, or TV shows.

roles (ROHLZ) Parts played by people in movies, plays, or TV shows.

science-fiction (sy-unts-FIK-shun) Work that deals with the effects of real or imagined science.

specialized (SPEH-shuh-lyzd) Did something very well.

thriller (THRIH-ler) A movie with action, adventure, and mystery.

Index

Due to the changing nature of Internet links, PowerKids Press has developed an online list of Web sites related to the subject of this book. This site is updated regularly. Please use this link to access the list: www.powerkidslinks.com/mss/depp/